SPIRIT & TRUTH

DEVOTED TO WORSHIP

Damon Stuart

Spirit & Truth: Devoted to Worship
Copyright © 2015 by Damon Stuart Ministries
damonstuart.com

ISBN: 978-0-692-47002-2

Printed in the USA by IngramSpark

Dedication & Acknowledgments

This book is dedicated to those who love to worship God and come before His presence with a song in their heart towards Him. There is nothing more fulfilling than being in the presence of our Lord and King. I pray this book will be one of those tools to help draw you into that intimate place with Jesus Christ.

To my wife and two teenage kids, thank you for your support, patience and understanding in supporting the ministry God has called me to steward. The journey at times has not always been easy but God will always reward those who diligently seek Him. Greater days are ahead because He is faithful!

Thank you to my parents and sisters for your encouragement and love. I'm very blessed to have been raised in such a loving family that has such a long and deep Christian heritage.

To my ministry board: Apostle Al Forniss, Pastor Vance Murphy, Pastor Terry Anderson, Apostle Diane Nutt and my father, Pastor V.O. Stuart. You have not only been strong and anointed leaders in my life but I'm honored to call you my closest friends. Thank you so very much for the many prayers and encouraging words during this project and over the past several years.

I want to especially thank those who prayerfully and financially helped make this book a reality. (*In Alphabetical Order*: Sandra Armstrong, Dr. Mark Barclay, Gerta Beck, Robert Butler, Cheryl Coots, Dolly Karadimos, Matt Lee, Suzanne Leto, Diane Lohmann, Chris Marczuk, Daryl Merrill Jr., Talisa Evans Newton, Ben & Brenda Peters, Theresa Phillips and Gloria Putnam)

Special recognition and thanks to my wife and to Pat Penn who read over, corrected and suggested the changes that were needed prior to this book going to print.

Most importantly, I have to thank my best friend and personal savior, Jesus Christ. It's because of all that He has done in my life that any of this is even happening. I'm so grateful for the promise He made to me the day I gave my life to Him—that this journey would be the greatest adventure I've ever been on and it surely has been that!

Endorsements

Spirit and Truth by Damon Stuart is a wonderful and refreshing look at worship in both the Old and New Testaments. With fresh insights from his own times of intimate worship, Damon has given us bite-sized nuggets of inspiration and encouragement that can be read over and over again. This book also makes a wonderful gift for a family member or friend. It will be a blessing to anyone who picks it up and reads it.

Ben R Peters
Co-Founder of Kingdom Sending Center
Author and International Bible Teacher
kingdomsendingcenter.org

"Do you want to jump start each day in the presence of God? Grab a copy of Damon's book and dive in."

Pastor Daryl Merrill Jr.
Christian Life Church
christianlifechurch.org

The Presence of God is the most needed manifestation in a believer's life. Through the devotions in Damon Stuart's book, the daily nuggets shared will lead and guide you to accessing more of God's Presence in your life through worship. There is a wealth of scripture in this book containing subjects such as faith, miracles, fearing the Lord, praise & worship, doing His will and trusting God. Damon's insight shared will lead you as the reader to a greater insight of what it means to worship God in spirit and truth. I've known Damon for many years and I still remember the 1st time we talked. As we began to share our hearts in spirit and truth, the Presence of God consumed us. I thought to myself…finally someone who really gets this….I have met a true worshiper! I recommend Damon's book to those who are yearning for a more intimate relationship with Him and desires to be one that worship's God in spirit and truth daily.

Apostle Diane Nutt
Speaker, Author & Counselor
dove-ministries.com

Foreword

I've been involved in Christian music leadership all of my adult life, some 40 years now. The last half of that has been as an itinerant worship leader that by the promotion of God has allowed me to travel the world, ministering on every continent, most of them numerous times. One thing is common throughout all of the many styles and experiences of worship I have observed, God is still seeking those who will worship Him in spirit and truth; and true worshipers are still seeking Him with all their hearts. Some things never change and this is good.

Worship is eternal. It's not an event or an occupation of Heaven—it's what Heaven's all about! We have the privilege and responsibility of practicing eternity's focus while still here on the earth. And we are the ones who get the biggest reward. I am the happiest and most at peace when I am worshiping the Lamb. It's why He made us, to give love away and receive love back. What a joy to fulfill our highest calling in life.

The key element of worship is the heart. It's all that Jesus cared about when He walked the earth and all He cares about today. That's why I like this manual, because I know the author. Damon Stuart has a worshiper's heart. I've known Damon for several years and every time we're together the same thing comes shining through in our conversations, his heart to love His Lord. It's from that place that he gives us these nuggets on worship. I hope you can sense the humility of Damon's heart, for it's there in every page. As you make your journey through this book, allow the great Teacher we know as the Holy Spirit to minister truth and life to you. Ask Him to give you a heart like David...a man after God's own heart. That's my prayer for you as well as for me. That's why this book is so timely for today and eternity. Enjoy the read!

Terry MacAlmon
Recording Artist & International Worship Leader
newglory.org

But the hour is coming, and now is, when the true worshipers will worship the Father in spirit and truth; for the Father is seeking such to worship Him. God *is* Spirit and those who worship Him must worship in spirit and truth."

John 4:23-24 (NKJV)

Day One

"Create in me a clean heart, O God, and renew a steadfast spirit within me. Do not cast me away from Your presence, And do not take Your Holy Spirit from me." (Psalms 51:10-11)

David was a man after God's own heart. We know this because even Paul states this very truth in Acts 13:22. After removing Saul, he made David their king. God testified concerning him: "I have found David son of Jesse, a man after my own heart; he will do everything I want him to do."

We also know about David as a shepherd who killed wild animals in protecting the sheep but also during this time he was a true worshiper and a psalmist in the making. Later he would be appointed by God to rule as King in Israel. David is known, loved and remembered by many around the world still today.

However, there is one thing about David that shows us the core of who he is in God, maintaining that place of brokenness and/or repentance. I believe that David shows us in these two verses, his way, of staying close to the heartbeat of God. He knew that it was more than just being clean; he knew that he had to stay in the presence of God through the Holy Spirit.

We all struggle from time to time with sin; doubt, anxiety, or even the plan God has for our lives which can lead us in other directions. Today I want to encourage you to ask God to give you a clean heart from everything. It doesn't necessarily mean that you are away from God; you just want Him to give you His heart for today! Ask the Holy Spirit to come and fill you fresh and new again. Worship God for how great He is despite what your mind is saying. God's mind is already made up about you anyway and it's always for your good. Only God can satisfy your soul so let Him come and surround you with His presence today.

Day Two

Then Jesus answered and said to her, "O woman, great is your faith! Let it be to you as you desire." And her daughter was healed from that very hour. (Matthew 15:28)

There is a classic, powerful hymn entitled "Great is Thy Faithfulness" that many sing today. While the song is a strong reminder of who God is in the midst of our situations, the question I ask is how great is our faith towards God?

That's what I love about this passage in Matthew 15. Jesus is healing the children of Israel and a Gentile woman is, by faith, pursuing the healing power of Jesus. At first He just ignored her. Kind of surprising since we all have this perception that Jesus is love and would never turn away from anyone crying out to Him. Even the disciples were annoyed with her, typical reaction from them, but she persists and falls on her knees before Jesus and begs for Him to help her.

Jesus throws this statement directly to her, "It is not good to take the children's bread and throw it to the little dogs." Take notice, this wasn't a lie spoken to her by the enemy, friends around her who didn't believe in miracles, or even her own thoughts, this was Jesus, the Son of God making this statement to her.

But she quickly responds to Him with this, "Yes, Lord, yet even the little dogs eat the crumbs which fall from their masters' table." Wow, I love it. She wasn't deterred from the belief that there was only one answer to her dire situation and that was through Jesus himself. Jesus responds so graciously to her because of the great faith she had towards Him. She simply believed and she wasn't going to settle for anything else.

Even today, both Jews and Gentiles have access to the Father through Jesus Christ and the same healing power then is still available today. How great is our faith towards Him? I believe that Jesus is the healer and that He is the same yesterday, today and forever. Great is His faithfulness because He loves us so much and desires that we live in complete health both physically and spiritually.

Day Three

But Jesus said, "Somebody touched Me, for I perceived power going out from Me." (Luke 8:46)

One morning, as I was reading this chapter and came to this particular verse, I immediately started to sing that classic song "He Touched Me." I love that line in the song that says *"And Oh the joy that floods my soul / something happened and now I know / He touched me and made me whole."*

As we read this passage from verses 43-48, we see a woman who had an issue of blood who is doing everything she can to touch Jesus. She has a physical ailment that no doctor or medicine can cure and is considered an outcast because of the Law of Moses. A perfect prescription for Jesus to show how much the Father loves His people by doing the impossible.

I am moved by the fact that she was so determined to get her healing. It didn't matter how many people stood in her way, the Law of Moses, complaining to God about her situation or even fear itself, she was set on her mission. She was focused, believing that her healing was going to happen through Jesus.

Are you walking around with issues today? Do you need a miraculous touch from God? Then I encourage you to seek the Lord diligently, not religiously, with a faith like this woman in Luke 8. To do anything and everything to touch the hem of His garment and receive the miracle you desperately need.

Jesus says to the crowd after the woman touched Him, "Who touched Me?" Of course no one wanted to say anything at first but then the woman speaks up and says that it was her and that she was healed IMMEDIATELY! His response to her was *"Be of good cheer, your faith has made you whole!"*

I don't know about you, but I want God to say to us as we press in for more of Him, "*Did you touch me today?*" I want our reply to be, Yes Lord; it was and we're so glad that you IMMEDIATELY moved in our lives and situations. And what will be His response to us be when we touch Him with our worship and our faith? "*Be of good cheer, your faith has made you well...Go in peace.*" Amen!

Day Four

So Jesus answered and said to them, "Assuredly, I say to you, if you have faith and do not doubt, you will not only do what was done to the fig tree, but also if you say to this mountain, 'Be removed and be cast into the sea,' it will be done. And whatever things you ask in prayer, believing, you will receive." (Matthew 21:21-22)

While it's easy to sing about faith, talk about faith or read about faith the bottom line is that faith is only real when we put it to action. The Bible says (James 2:20) that "faith without works is dead!" So as we read the Bible and study the words and actions of Jesus in the four gospels, as born again believers, we have been given the same faith and power in us because we serve a mighty God.

My prayer has been, Lord, give me faith today to move mountains so I may fulfill your purposes and plans for my life and expand the kingdom of heaven here on the earth. I encourage you today to put into action the instructions given to us by Jesus in the four gospels and the book of Acts, that we would have the power of faith to move mountains out of our way.

Do you need faith for a miracle? Then begin to worship Jesus today. Spend time with Him and begin to pray, believing you will receive because it's already yours through the blood and sacrifice that Jesus made on the cross. You can do all things through Jesus Christ and I believe you will have faith to move mountains and as He moves on your behalf just give Him the glory for it.

Day Five

"For whatever is born of God overcomes the world. And this is the victory that has overcome the world-our faith. Who is he who overcomes the world, but he who believes that Jesus is the Son of God?" (1 John 5:4-5)

As a Christian, you are a child of God, a son and daughter of the King and you have the power through Jesus to conquer the world because of faith. This is the power that God has given to each of us to reveal the kingdom of God to the world that is looking for salvation.

This is the cry that is going forth from the four corners of the earth. Where is the salvation of the Lord? It's in you, the believer, to make yourself available to be the voice, representative and ambassador of the Lord most High! God has not given us the spirit of fear but of power, love and sound mind to do as Jesus did when he walked on the earth. We are to go about sharing the good news of Jesus Christ, demonstrating the heart of the Father with signs and wonders following. The world is searching to know God and they do believe in the miraculous because they run after so many false ones.

Here is the reality, time is running short on the earth and we all have a mission and a calling to proclaim the good news, that Jesus Christ is the only way. It's not a religious thing, it's a relationship thing! The illusion for too many has been that "I can't really do anything for God" or "That's just for those who have been called into ministry." That my friend is a lie from the enemy, as you are more than qualified to win people to Christ the moment you became born again.

We all can do many miraculous things through Jesus Christ. I know because He said so in His word. His word says that if my faith is as big as mustard seed, I could move mountains. The faith it took for you to become saved is the same amount of faith needed to win others to Christ and see the power of miracles operate in your life. God desires so much for us to walk in the same power and authority that Jesus did that He made the criteria of our faith like the size of a mustard seed so we would easily believe.

If you need more faith today look no further because I believe John gives us the perfect answer to ask God for more. Let's again look at this chapter reading verses 14-15:

14 Now this is the confidence that we have in Him, that if we ask anything according to His will, He hears us.
15 And if we know that He hears us, whatever we ask, we know that we have the petitions that we have asked of Him.

There is our answer today for more faith and for other things as well when we pray and ask God for help. Believe me; He's more ready to move on your behalf than you are. I want to encourage and provoke you to the place of desiring more faith and see the lost come into the kingdom of God in record numbers. As John said, this is the confidence that we have in Him when we ask for anything in His will. I believe that His will for you and me is that we would be the ones who say "Here am I Lord, send me."

Day Six

"Go, gather all the Jews who are present in Shushan, and fast for me; neither eat nor drink for three days, night or day. My maids and I will fast likewise. And so I will go to the king, which is against the law; and if I perish, I perish!" (Esther 4:16)

FASTING! Not a word many of us like to hear, including myself. However, it is something I try to do when the Lord is really pulling me in that direction. One day as I was praying the Lord was drawing me to several different passages in the Bible about fasting. I came to Esther 4 because it's a type of fast that I do more regularly then other types of fasting.

I do need to preface that everyone has different ways and types of fasting and no one way is better or greater than another. It's really what the Lord lays on your heart to do at that time. There are times when things become so overwhelming that you just know that a certain type of fast is needed to see the breakthrough or answers from God.

As you read this chapter in Esther, they needed a breakthrough with an answer to their dire situation quickly. It says in chapter three that Haman sought to destroy all the Jews who were throughout the whole kingdom of Ahasuerus—the people of Mordecai. When this was found out by Mordecai, he went to Esther to tell her what the plan was against God's people and pleaded with her to go before the King on their behalf.

As many of you know the story, she and all of those around her went into a three day fast for this overwhelming situation. By chapter seven her petition to the King is heard and is granted so that the Jews are saved from the evil plan of destruction. Praise the Lord!

In the New Testament, we know that Jesus went up into the mountain after being baptized by John and fasted for forty days. There He was tempted by the enemy but Jesus won and overcame. In Matthew 6, Jesus talks about fasting and says this key statement: "Moreover, when you fast..." Now as you know, Jesus is referring to the point about "when" and not "if or maybe" on fasting. Fasting is essential in our walk with God. Some may do it more than others but we all need to fast from time to time.

Why should you fast? The answer is simple; it's really about drawing closer to God. Fasting breaks off the stuff that usually keeps us sometimes from hearing the Lord more clearly. It also reveals the heart issues that perhaps you didn't even know you had and it even causes your worship to touch Him deeper in ways you didn't even know you could.

Jesus also touched on fasting regarding miracles. In Mark 9, Jesus delivers a boy who was both deaf and mute from an unclean spirit because the disciples could not. In verse 29, He makes this powerful and valuable statement to them and to us today: "This kind can come out by nothing but prayer and fasting."

We know that prayer is not only important, but should be a daily essential part of our lives. I want to encourage you that fasting is also an essential part of our walk with God as is prayer, worship and reading the Word. If you need a breakthrough or miracle today then you know what you need to do. Just ask the Lord what type of fast you should do for the situation that you're facing today. You will not only see the breakthrough victory come like Esther did but you will also have a deeper connection with Jesus like never before.

Day Seven

And Jesus said to him, "I will come and heal him." (Matthew 8:7)

As you read the entire chapter of Matthew 8, you will quickly notice that it is full of accounts of Jesus doing extraordinary miracles. From healings, calming the sea to casting out a legion of demons from a man into pigs, it is a marvelous glimpse of the power and love of Jesus Christ.

The one passage I want to draw your attention to is from verses 5-13 of this chapter. Here we have a Roman centurion, a captain, who comes pleading for help to a Jew, Jesus himself. He even goes on to make the statement to Jesus that "I am not worthy that You should come under my roof" which is startling when you actually understand the times that this is written in since the Romans were the occupying force in Jerusalem. I love how the Bible says Jesus reacted to this: When Jesus heard it, He marveled, and said to those who followed, "Assuredly, I say to you, I have not found such great faith, not even in Israel!"

All human factors go out the window when you are truly desperate for a miracle, which this man was. When you need a miracle, you no longer worry about your pride, proper etiquette, religious affiliations or denominations, etc... No, you just need God to show up and do something because there is no backup plan.

That's why we hear so often about the miracles that takes place so often and so big overseas because the majority of people there have no plan B, plan C and so on. They don't have doctors, hospitals, insurance or even much money in most cases. All they have is faith to believe that Jesus Christ is the healer and the only answer!

Please take a moment to read it and meditate on Matthew 8:5-13 from the Message Bible. Place yourself there in that moment and ask

20

God to give you that type of faith like the centurion. Knowing that all God has to do is just speak the word—and it is done.

Matthew 8:5-13 (The Message)

5-6 As Jesus entered the village of Capernaum, a Roman captain came up in a panic and said, "Master, my servant is sick. He can't walk. He's in terrible pain."

7 Jesus said, "I'll come and heal him."

8-9 "Oh, no," said the captain. "I don't want to put you to all that trouble. Just give the order and my servant will be fine. I'm a man who takes orders and gives orders. I tell one soldier, 'Go,' and he goes; to another, 'Come,' and he comes; to my slave, 'Do this,' and he does it."

10-12 Taken aback, Jesus said, "I've yet to come across this kind of simple trust in Israel, the very people who are supposed to know all about God and how he works. This man is the vanguard of many outsiders who will soon be coming from all directions— streaming in from the east, pouring in from the west, sitting down at God's kingdom banquet alongside Abraham, Isaac, and Jacob. Then those who grew up 'in the faith' but had no faith will find themselves out in the cold, outsiders to grace and wondering what happened."

13 Then Jesus turned to the captain and said, "Go. What you believed could happen has happened." At that moment his servant became well.

Day Eight

Now when they began to sing and to praise, the LORD set ambushes against the people of Ammon, Moab, and Mount Seir, who had come against Judah; and they were defeated.
(2 Chronicles 20:22)

There's an old song we used to sing in church that went like this: "Let God arise and let His enemies be scattered, let God, let God arise!" That's what I want to encourage you with today. As King Jehoshaphat and Israel faced annihilation from their enemies, they sought after the heart of God and saw their enemies defeated. Let's examine through the word how they responded to their conflict and how God moved on their behalf.

2 Chronicles 20:15-25:

15 And he said, "Listen, all you of Judah and you inhabitants of Jerusalem, and you, King Jehoshaphat! Thus says the LORD to you: 'Do not be afraid nor dismayed because of this great multitude, for the battle is not yours, but God's.

16 Tomorrow go down against them. They will surely come up by the Ascent of Ziz, and you will find them at the end of the brook before the Wilderness of Jeruel.

17 You will not need to fight in this battle. Position yourselves, stand still and see the salvation of the LORD, who is with you, O Judah and Jerusalem!' Do not fear or be dismayed; tomorrow go out against them, for the LORD is with you."

18 And Jehoshaphat bowed his head with his face to the ground, and all Judah and the inhabitants of Jerusalem bowed before the LORD, worshiping the LORD.

19 Then the Levites of the children of the Kohathites and of the children of the Korahites stood up to praise the LORD God of Israel with voices loud and high.

20 So they rose early in the morning and went out into the Wilderness of Tekoa; and as they went out, Jehoshaphat stood and said, "Hear me, O Judah and you inhabitants of Jerusalem: Believe in the LORD your God, and you shall be established; believe His prophets, and you shall prosper."

21 And when he had consulted with the people, he appointed those who should sing to the LORD, and who should praise the beauty of holiness, as they went out before the army and were saying:

"Praise the LORD, For His mercy endures forever."

22 Now when they began to sing and to praise, the LORD set ambushes against the people of Ammon, Moab, and Mount Seir, who had come against Judah; and they were defeated.

23 For the people of Ammon and Moab stood up against the inhabitants of Mount Seir to utterly kill and destroy them. And when they had made an end of the inhabitants of Seir, they helped to destroy one another.

24 So when Judah came to a place overlooking the wilderness, they looked toward the multitude; and there were their dead bodies, fallen on the earth. No one had escaped.

25 When Jehoshaphat and his people came to take away their spoil, they found among them an abundance of valuables on the dead bodies, and precious jewelry, which they stripped off for themselves, more than they could carry away; and they were three days gathering the spoil because there was so much.

So we see here that God is the one who goes before us and delivers us from all of our enemies. The keys in this passage are:

1. Do not be afraid or be dismayed for the battle is not yours (verse 15)

2. You do not need to fight—Just position yourself in the Lord (verse 17)

3. Worship the Lord! (verses 18-19)

4. Believe God and His prophets (the Word) and you will prosper and be established (verse 20)

5. Sing the Song of the Lord into your situation and He will defeat your enemies (verses 22-24)

6. God will give you victory—with spoils left over! (verse 25)

Praise and worship is just more than singing a song to God. It's full of heavenly power that can and will change the atmosphere when you set your heart towards Him. The enemy is more afraid of you then you think because you have the power and God tools to destroy his work and assignments that are against you. Let God Arise!

Day Nine

"Let everything that has breathe praise the LORD."
(Psalm 150:6)

We were created to praise and worship the Lord. The Bible reveals to us from Genesis to Revelation the call to worship God, the power of praise, and what all in heaven are doing as John witnessed the worship around the throne. No matter where you are, what you're doing today, take a few minutes to praise God for who He is. A friend of mine once said, as Christians, we were called to be environmentalists. As we go to work or school each day, the environment we're in is depending upon us to reveal the glory and majesty of the King. Praise Him and change your environment today!

Psalm 150 (The Message)

Hallelujah! Praise God in his holy house of worship,
> *praise him under the open skies;*
Praise him for his acts of power,
> *praise him for his magnificent greatness;*
Praise with a blast on the trumpet,
> *praise by strumming soft strings;*
Praise him with castanets and dance,
> *praise him with banjo and flute;*
Praise him with cymbals and a big bass drum,
> *praise him with fiddles and mandolin.*
Let every living, breathing creature praise God!
> *Hallelujah!*

Day Ten

Then Elijah said to Ahab, "Go up, eat and drink; for there is the sound of abundance of rain." (1 Kings 18:41)

As I read this one morning, this particular verse and passage leapt from the page to me. It felt like the Holy Spirit was drawing me right to verses 41-46, especially with verse 41 which says "for there is the sound of abundance of rain." As I read that I immediately remembered what it says in Acts 2:1-2 which reads:

1 When the Day of Pentecost had fully come, they were all with one accord in one place. 2 And suddenly "there came a sound" from heaven, as of a rushing mighty wind, and it filled the whole house where they were sitting.

So what is God saying and doing with this word "sound" from these two separate but yet powerful events that happened in the Old and New Testament? By definition, sound is a travelling wave which is an oscillation of pressure transmitted through a solid, liquid, or gas, composed of frequencies within the range of hearing and of a level sufficiently strong to be heard, or the sensation stimulated in organs of hearing by such vibrations.

It has been scientifically stated that once a person says something, the sound of your words continues on out into space forever. Can you imagine the worship that has gone on for thousands of years to God that is still being heard in Heaven? Another scientific report was released that the sun sends out musical waves from the flares that continue to erupt. The Bible says that even the rocks would cry out if no one would, so now we have scientific evidence that music (sound) is very important in the Kingdom of God. Praise the Lord!

As I meditated on this verse about the sound of abundance of rain, I knew that the Lord was speaking to me that we have been in a time when darkness has increased upon the earth and that God's people are under much stress because of the wickedness of the land but God will have the final say!

I believe the Lord is saying that if we will humble ourselves in prayer as Elijah did in this passage and worship declaring that "The Lord, He is God" we will see the clouds begin to form, take shape and God will send the rain of salvation and miracles. As Elijah told Ahab to prepare his chariot, I believe that God is saying to us today that we need to prepare for the abundance of what God is about to do in His people for such a time as this. I strongly sense that the Lord will gird us up to run ahead like Elijah to see the greatest outpouring of His spirit on our nation, cities, homes, churches and those around us for the kingdom and for the glory of God!

I want to hear the sound of heaven, the sound of abundance and the sound of the rushing mighty wind from the Lord so that the gospel will go forth in power and that the four corners of the earth will be filled with the glory of God! I pray that all the nations would have an encounter with Jesus Christ and that the sound we release unto Him through true and pure worship would be such a sweet, sweet sound unto His ears today!

Day Eleven

Then David said to the Philistine, "You come to me with a sword, with a spear, and with a javelin. But I come to you in the name of the LORD of hosts, the God of the armies of Israel, whom you have defied. This day the LORD will deliver you into my hand..." (1 Samuel 17:45-46)

I love how David was confident in the Lord, even in his youth. Many of you know the story of David taking on Goliath and defeating him with a stone and slingshot. What I want to share with you is just a reminder that there will be times when we will be facing a giant in our lives. From finances, jobs, health, spiritual warfare, addictions or even family crisis, there will be giants that we will have to overcome.

The problem with the army of Israel in this passage is that they kept their focus on the giant itself instead of focusing on how God was going to give them victory by delivering the giant into their hands. They allowed fear to take hold so the worship unto God couldn't be released and God could not move on their behalf. But God is so good, that He would orchestrate it so David's father, Jesse, would send him to check on his brothers. God's plans are greater because they always surprise you and especially the enemy.

David had to be used because he was a true worshiper but also because he wasn't in the camp with the army where fear had gotten a hold. David had taken on a lion and a bear so he knew he had to take on giants in his natural life. God had already been grooming him as he spent hours alone tending to the flocks, meditating and worshiping the Lord. David truly understood the audience of one mentality with the King of kings which was preparing him to be a real king later in his life.

As you read this, do not let the giants you are facing dictate to you who you are going to be and what your circumstances are. As David rose up against Goliath, he spoke with faith and authority when he said "I come to you in the name of the LORD of hosts, the God of the armies of Israel, whom you have defied. This day the LORD will deliver you into my hand…" As you worship the Lord today, rise up with the same authority that has been given to you through Jesus Christ and declare to your giants that this day, "The Lord will deliver me and that I am more than conqueror in Jesus name". Praise the Lord for He is worthy!

Day Twelve

"For You, O God, have tested us; You have refined us as silver is refined." (Psalm 66:10)

If I took a survey and asked how many would like to be tested and go through trials, I'm sure it would be a zero response.

Today, you may be going through one of the hardest times ever. Many of us know the verses that we "should count it all joy when going through trials" and so on. But lets' face it; sometimes we don't want verses, prayers, and Christian jargon responses to the stuff we're going through. We want a pity party and we want everyone around us to be in agreement with us while we're hosting that party. Am I right?

I know that I'm not alone because we have all been there and done it. It's easy to get burdened or overwhelmed to the point that nothing seems to work or nothing is happening. But let me remind you today, God is working and moving on your behalf, even right now! That party you want to have is because your flesh, along with enemies prodding and assignments against you, is the sign that things are about to change and that God has been working diligently for you behind the scenes.

Remember when Daniel in the Old Testament was praying for an answer and it took the angel of the Lord twenty-one days to get to Daniel and the angel said that "on the first day, the Lord heard your prayer!" Believe me, God has heard your cry and prayer on the first day, sometimes there is just a delay in getting the answer.

I love this chapter in Psalms; particularly verse ten because David says "For you, O God, have tested us; and You have refined us as silver." Many of you know the analogy about the process a silver smith goes through in making silver. As the silver is being heated into the shape that it's going to become, the heat removes the dross (impurities) from the metal so it becomes flawless. What you may not know is that the heating process has to be perfect, it can't be too hot or minute portions of silver will be carried off with the lead and if not hot enough it will be found that it has been imperfectly performed, and the silver will not have entirely freed itself from the base metals. There is a knowing perfection by the refiner before and during the refining process.

A perfect example from the New Testament by one of the greatest Apostles is Paul. As you read through the book of Acts you see the transformation (refining) that the Lord takes him through. After Paul's arrest in Acts 21, Paul is taken on an incredible journey by the Lord. Paul is "tried" before several Roman authority figures and it's only when he petitions his case to go to Rome that his being "tried" turns into a "witness!"

You see, when Paul came through all of the fiery trials and tests, he was proved and refined because he had been "tried." When you have come through those things, you then become the "witness" of Jesus Christ here on the earth. You will reflect the pure heart of Christ and do even greater things than He did because you have been refined by the Holy Spirit.

At this time, when you feel like the problems are bigger than you and you want to have that pity party, just remember Paul. While your problems may seem big at the moment and the answers you seek are important, are you going to party with your pity or are you going to become a witness to those that God has put in and around your life today?

I don't know about you but I'm want to be refined by God and want to be one that was "tried" and "refined" and then became a powerful "witness" for the kingdom of God and declare that our God is greater!

Day Thirteen

"The fear of the LORD is the beginning of wisdom; a good understanding have all those who do His commandments. His praise endures forever." (Psalm 111:10)

"The FEAR of the LORD is the beginning"....Powerful words to end chapter 111 of Psalms, which is really a praise regarding God's incredible care for us. What is this "FEAR" of the Lord that we read or hear from the scriptures? You may be reading this and already know but sometimes it's always good to get a good reminder since we tend to forget, we are human. I believe that we need to stay at a place of holy reverence unto God. Yes, God is love and He bestows great grace upon us. We have incredible freedom and joy in the Holy Spirit but He's also God almighty, the creator of heaven and earth that moves and operates in amazing power by just a word being spoken. I believe that if we have a heart and attitude of Godly fear then we are definitely going to be used greatly for the kingdom.

So what is the fear of the Lord? Here is one definition I came across which states: "For the unbeliever, the fear of God is the fear of the judgment of God and eternal death, which is eternal separation from God. For the believer, the fear of God is something much different. The believer's fear of God is total REVERENCE of God. There is the convergence of awe, adoration, honor, worship, confidence, thankfulness, love, and, yes, fear."

There are several great scriptures on the "fear of the Lord" from a biblical perspective that I want to share with you below so that you can have a deeper understanding of "the fear of God" but I also want you to know that it's one of the gifts of the Holy Spirit, as described in Isaiah 11:2-3:

32

The Spirit of the LORD shall rest upon Him, the Spirit of wisdom and understanding, the Spirit of counsel and might, the Spirit of knowledge and of the fear of the LORD. His delight is in the fear of the LORD, and He shall not judge by the sight of His eyes, nor decide by the hearing of His ears;

Verses on Those Who Fear the LORD:

Proverbs 1:7—The fear of the LORD is the beginning of knowledge.

Proverbs 8:13—The fear of the LORD is to hate evil. Pride and arrogance and the evil way, and the perverted mouth, I hate.

Proverbs 9:10—The fear of the LORD is the beginning of wisdom, and the knowledge of the Holy One is understanding.

Proverbs 10:27—The fear of the LORD prolongs life, but the years of the wicked will be shortened.

Proverbs14:26—In the fear of the LORD there is strong confidence, and his children will have refuge.

Proverbs 14:27—The fear of the LORD is a fountain of life, that one may avoid the snares of death.

Proverbs 15:16—Better is a little with the fear of the LORD, than great treasure and turmoil with it.

Proverbs 15:33—The fear of the LORD is the instruction for wisdom, and before honor [comes] humility.

Proverbs 16:6—By loving-kindness and truth iniquity is atoned for, and by the fear of the LORD one keeps away from evil.

Proverbs 19:23—The fear of the LORD [leads] to life, so that one may sleep satisfied, untouched by evil.

Proverbs 22:4—The reward of humility [and] the fear of the LORD are riches, honor and life.

Proverbs 23:17—But [live] in the fear of the LORD always. Do not let your heart envy sinners…

Day Fourteen

As He prayed, the appearance of His face was altered, and His robe became white and glistening. (Luke 9:29)

I am continuously fascinated on how God moves and operates. From this chapter, there have been many sermons and articles written on the "Mountain of Transfiguration" so I am not here to add some great revelation but really just a personal observation.

When it says in verse 29 "As He prayed, the appearance of His face was altered," that just spoke volumes to me about the power of prayer. How often do we pray? When we do pray, is it the will, desires and heart of God or is it the long list of petitions and/or complaints? Praying is not only required to live a Christian life, it is vital for your spiritual health, growth and success in the kingdom. It's not really an option but it should be just as important and regular as eating 3 meals a day in your life. I want to encourage you to pray and pray in the spirit even more as that is the greatest weapon that we have through the Holy Spirit.

Jesus understood that the miracles and all that He did while He was on the earth came from spending time in prayer early in the morning with the Father. If He did it and it was important and He was the Son of God, how much more is it for us today? Believe me when I tell you that the more you pray and spend time with God YOUR appearance will be altered and you will become that witness of Jesus Christ to the world. Those around you will know that you are God's beloved son or daughter and they will hear you and you can minister to them because they see the glory of the Lord upon you.

Below, you will see Luke 9:27-36 and as you read it, ask the Holy Spirit to show you how to pray effectively. Meditate on verse 29. Praying is so much more than just making requests; it's the communication line between you and God that will cause you to have a "transfiguration" in your own life.

²⁷ *"But I tell you truly, there are some standing here who shall not taste death till they see the kingdom of God."*

²⁸ *Now it came to pass, about eight days after these sayings, that He took Peter, John, and James and went up on the mountain to pray.*

²⁹ *As He prayed, the appearance of His face was altered, and His robe became white and glistening.*

³⁰ *And behold, two men talked with Him, who were Moses and Elijah,*

³¹ *who appeared in glory and spoke of His decease which He was about to accomplish at Jerusalem.*

³² *But Peter and those with him were heavy with sleep; and when they were fully awake, they saw His glory and the two men who stood with Him.*

³³ *Then it happened, as they were parting from Him, that Peter said to Jesus, "Master, it is good for us to be here; and let us make three tabernacles: one for You, one for Moses, and one for Elijah"— not knowing what he said.*

³⁴ *While he was saying this, a cloud came and overshadowed them; and they were fearful as they entered the cloud.*

³⁵ *And a voice came out of the cloud, saying, "This is My beloved Son. Hear Him!"*

³⁶ *When the voice had ceased, Jesus was found alone. But they kept quiet, and told no one in those days any of the things they had seen.*

Day Fifteen

"He who dwells in the secret place of the Most High shall abide under the shadow of the Almighty. I will say of the LORD, He is my refuge and my fortress; my God, in Him I will trust." (Psalms 91:1-2)

This passage and chapter is one that many Christians know and love from the book of Psalms. David was such a gifted and anointed writer of his day and that's why these verses are still as powerful today as they were then.

I love the very first part of these verses that says *"He who dwells in the secret place of the Most High shall abide under the shadow of the Almighty."* I don't know about you but my greatest desire and prayer is to dwell daily in the secret place with God. David understood what it meant to run to God in the midst of his battles and fears, praying and crying out that, without God, his life would be over. He knew that only God could save and protect him in the midst of life's chaos, battles and hardships. God's secret place is always a place of safety!

Let's read these two verses again but now from the Message Bible:

You who sit down in the High God's presence, spend the night in Shaddai's shadow and say this: "God, you're my refuge. I trust in you and I'm safe!"

What a comfort to know that God is our hiding place and safe refuge in our time of trouble. But He is not just there for us during those times, He is there also when we want to spend time with Him in fellowship through worship. There is that secret place that He desires us to come to, when we learn to put away our many requests and lists and just spend time with the one who first loved us. I encourage you today to rest and dwell with the Father and thank Him for that He has done, even for the things you don't even know that He did. He loves you and desires you to become a true son and daughter that will trust in Him no matter what the situation is that you are facing today.

There's a song titled "Have Your Way" by Darlene Zschech who was one of the worship leaders from Hillsong Church Australia. This song has been around for some time now but the words are powerful. I highly recommend you add it to your worship playlist if you haven't already. Take in the words of the song and let them become your hearts cry to God to let Him have His way in your life today!

Day Sixteen

But at midnight Paul and Silas were praying and singing hymns to God, and the prisoners were listening to them. (Acts 16:25)

Praise and worship is what we all were created to do! Everyone on the earth since Adam and Eve has worshiped something or has been searching for God to worship. There are those who have trivialized the need for worship in church services to actual worship wars based on the types of worship that must be sung in our services.

I have encountered some church leaders who even say that worship as we know and do today is not God's plan but a deception of the enemy since worship wasn't instructed specifically by Jesus under the new covenant. The enemy has so targeted the understanding of true worship that we now have all of these distractions among the brethren over what worship is, should be and so on. It's a plan that has worked well in many places and has even destroyed the lives and callings of some who were once worship leaders and/or pastors.

While all this may seem somewhat like a downer, the fact is, praise and worship over the last 15 years has exploded onto the earth like never before in history. Besides an ever increasing anointing for true worship upon God's people, the technology today has helped create a growing need for fresh new worship from heaven. From the cassette tape era, then CD's, iTunes and the internet, praise and worship has become so accessible to everyone all over the world. And now with sites like YouTube, the video side of praise and worship captured from live events is now changing the landscape of accessibility of being there as well.

As I was reading this passage, I meditated on this one scripture and kept thinking that if we, God's people, could place ourselves in Paul and Silas's situation, would we do as they did? After being beaten and thrown into prison, could you begin to pray & worship God as they did? I'm challenging myself as much as I'm challenging you.

There is something that I do take from it though. Despite the many worship songs and resources we have available to us, do I have a song in me that would move the Lord in a dire situation that even a great earthquake would take place? That's exactly what happens in the next verse when you read on in Acts 16:26—*"Suddenly there was a great earthquake, so that the foundations of the prison were shaken; and immediately all the doors were opened and everyone's chains were loosed."*

The power of praise of worship doesn't come from the flesh or soulish realm but from the spirit man that is inside of you. When you begin to worship God in "spirit and in truth"—that's the kind of worship the Father is seeking (John 4). Worship like this has an effect that not only answers your problems but becomes a powerful display and testimony of how great God is and loosens the chains of everyone around.

I have always said that the true power regarding praise and worship is that it changes the hearts and minds of men so that God gets to fulfill His plan and purposes beyond our expectations and limitations. When the power of God is released through the power of worship it also sets the stage for salvation via evangelism.

Later in the chapter, Paul and Silas share the gospel with the jailer and his family and his entire household become saved because of the power of God being displayed through true worship—which was offered up by just two men in a jail cell.

No matter what troubles, hardships or even prison you may be in today, if you can learn to pray and worship with a heart like Paul and Silas you will see God move and shake the foundations around you so that you will be set free from those chains. You will then have the opportunity to share the good news about Jesus to those around you who also see what the Lord has done.

Day Seventeen

"The LORD will give strength to His people; the LORD will bless His people with peace." (Psalm 29:11)

What an encouraging reminder from the word of God. God will strengthen you and bless you with His peace in the midst of your storms. David had such a unique life of adventure from herding sheep to winning great battles for King Saul to eventually becoming King of Israel. The journey for him was filled with ups and downs, good times and bad and even victories and losses. The main thing about David is that no matter what happened he always turned to the Lord either in prayerful desperation or in praise and thanksgiving, dancing before the Lord. There is so much about David we could learn from that could help us in becoming true worshipers ourselves.

The reason David makes this powerful statement of the promise of God in verse eleven is because he is revealing to us the powerful voice of God in his circumstances. When you read this entire chapter, the word "voice" appears seven times. Today, when we worship God, it requires our voice declaring the word of God and/or the words of our heart toward God. You cannot praise or worship the God of all creation in silence, it doesn't work.

Below is Psalm 29 from the Message Bible in its entirety. Take a few minutes to read it out loud today and let your circumstances or the storms in your life know that the "Voice of the Lord" is going to have the final say starting today. Amen!

Psalm 29 (The Message)

1-2 Bravo, God, bravo! Gods and all angels shout, "Encore!" In awe before the glory, in awe before God's visible power. Stand at attention! Dress your best to honor him!

3 God thunders across the waters, Brilliant, his voice and his face, streaming brightness—God, across the flood waters.

4 God's thunder tympanic, God's thunder symphonic.

5 God's thunder smashes cedars, God topples the northern cedars.

6 The mountain ranges skip like spring colts, the high ridges jump like wild kid goats.

7-8 God's thunder spits fire. God thunders, the wilderness quakes; He makes the desert of Kadesh shake.

9 God's thunder sets the oak trees dancing a wild dance, whirling; the pelting rain strips their branches. We fall to our knees—we call out, "Glory!"

10 Above the floodwaters is God's throne from which his power flows, from which he rules the world.

11 God makes his people strong. God gives his people peace.

Day Eighteen

"The LORD is near to those who have a broken heart, and saves such as have a contrite spirit." (Psalm 34:18)

I will be honest, there are times I get up in the morning and can't seem to pray. It's as though I'm praying against a brick wall the entire time. I'm sure many of you have felt the same when praying and it can be especially frustrating when you are in a crisis and/or needing that answer to the big situation that's in your life. Like me, you are probably facing some important decisions, opportunities, obstacles and more but I know that I am determined to seek the Lord to have Him direct my life and to show me His choices and plans for my life, which is not always easy.

When reading Psalm 34, this chapter is really David saying that in all things and in every situation in life—Just seek the Lord! Today's verse sums it up when David declares that *"The LORD is near to those who have a broken heart, and saves such as have a contrite spirit."* God is so near to all of us when we put our total trust in Him even when our flesh/mind says otherwise. I believe verse seven confirms this when it says *"The angel of the LORD encamps all around those who fear Him, and delivers them."*

When situations and obstacles become so large that you feel overwhelmed, it's time to run to God as David did in Psalms 34 and begin to worship Him with a broken heart and contrite spirit. He will show up on your behalf and prove to you that He is there for you because He loves you. Read Psalm 34 below in its entirety because the Word is powerful and it never returns void.

Psalm 34 (The Message)

¹ I bless God every chance I get; my lungs expand with his praise.

² I live and breathe God; if things aren't going well, hear this and be happy:

³ Join me in spreading the news; together let's get the word out.

⁴ God met me more than halfway, he freed me from my anxious fears.

⁵ Look at him; give him your warmest smile. Never hide your feelings from him.

⁶ When I was desperate, I called out, and God got me out of a tight spot.

⁷ God's angel sets up a circle of protection around us while we pray.

⁸ Open your mouth and taste, open your eyes and see—how good God is. Blessed are you who run to him.

⁹ Worship God if you want the best; worship opens doors to all his goodness.

¹⁰ Young lions on the prowl get hungry, but God-seekers are full of God.

¹¹ Come, children, listen closely; I'll give you a lesson in God worship.

¹² Who out there has a lust for life? Can't wait each day to come upon beauty?

Day Nineteen

And Ezra blessed the LORD, the great God. Then all the people answered, "Amen, Amen!" while lifting up their hands. And they bowed their heads and worshiped the LORD with their faces to the ground. (Nehemiah 8:6)

For some, reading the Old Testament can seem daunting at times, for example, when you read from some of the "minor" prophets it can seem tedious because of strange sounding names and lots of details. As we continue this walk and relationship with the Lord, I realize that God's Word is not only important for you or me to read just so we can be strong in the Lord but it actually brings us closer in relationship with Him.

When reading chapter 8 of Nehemiah, I was in awe of how the children of Israel reacted when Ezra (the scribe) stood up on a platform which in verse five says: *"And Ezra opened the book in the sight of all the people, for he was standing above all the people; and when he opened it, <u>all the people stood up.</u>"* When the book was opened, the people stood up in reverence to the Word of God being read. What an incredible picture we get as to the heart of how the people honored the God of Abraham, Isaac and Jacob.

As you get to verse nine, you do get to see a glimpse of their heart and attitude as it unfolds:

And Nehemiah, who was the governor, Ezra the priest and scribe, and the Levites who taught the people said to all the people, "This day is holy to the LORD your God; do not mourn nor weep." <u>For all the people wept, when they heard the words of the Law.</u>

And the verse finishes with "the people wept when they heard the word!" What I really find amazing is that after this verse he commands the people to go eat, refresh themselves and help those who cannot for this time is holy unto the Lord. Then he makes this incredible statement that many of us know today at the end of verse ten.

"Do not sorrow, for the joy of the LORD is your strength."

And the people went as they were told and rejoiced greatly because they "understood the words" that were declared to them.

The Word of God is not something that is supposed to be boring or religious. Reading God's Word is like eating food that sustains us continually, but even more than that, it's the heartbeat of who God is. If we say we want to know more of God, be like Him and win souls to Him, shouldn't we know Him so well that it would be easier to do all those things?

I believe that we should ask God everyday to make the Word come alive and that He would give us fresh revelation from His Word each time we read it. When we treasure the Word like the children of Israel did in these passages, we too will rejoice because we understand the precious life-giving words of our God—the one who gives us our strength.

Day Twenty

"For You, O LORD, will bless the righteous; with favor You will surround him as with a shield." (Psalms 5:12)

On one particular morning during the holidays, I was really struggling to pray because I was still very tired and sleepy. Having family come visit and stay with you is wonderful but you know that you never get the kind of rest you usually get when people are staying in your home.

I still got up, pressed in and prayed despite my fatigue and as I did I was reminding myself the importance of Morning Prayer with the Lord. It's not something that is a "routine" or a "religious" thing that we do, but it's part of that relationship with the Lord that we should always treasure deeply.

Let's take a look at Psalms chapter 5 because it's all about David going to God in the morning for guidance through prayer. I love what he says in verses 1-3 of this chapter:

[1] Give ear to my words, O LORD, consider my meditation.
[2] Give heed to the voice of my cry, my King and my God, for to You I will pray.
[3] My voice You shall hear in the morning, O LORD; in the morning I will direct it to You, and I will look up.

David is saying, "God, listen to my words and consider my heart towards you. In the morning I will give you my prayers and my worship and I will look to you alone!"

Worship is so vital in our walk and relationship with the Lord but I cannot stress enough the importance of daily, early Morning Prayer time with the Lord as well. What time each morning and for how long is between you and the Lord, but spending time with Him before your day begins is the most important thing you can do.

God can and will go before you, He will help you in your choices and decision making. He will give you wisdom, favor and lay a hedge of protection around you and much more because you spent time with Him and you have made that connection to Him through His spirit.

Prayer is an important way to spend relationship time with the one we love, our God! It's not just about giving Him our requests and petitions but asking God to make us more like Him each and every day. Let's read it now in its full context starting with the verse before it.

Psalms 5:11-12:

[11] But let all those rejoice who put their trust in You; let them ever shout for joy, because You defend them; Let those also who love Your name be joyful in You.
[12] For You, O LORD, will bless the righteous; with favor You will surround him as with a shield.

Day Twenty One

"For where your treasure is, there your heart will be also." (Luke 12:34) **"...For out of the abundance of the heart his mouth speaks."** (Luke 6:45b)

One day as I was reading in Luke, these two verses really popped out to me. Notice in both of these verses that it's about the heart. Everything with God has been and will always be about the heart of man having the heart of the Father.

This was the very plan since creation and even more so when Jesus died on the cross for our sins—so that we would allow Him into our hearts. The heart of God is about fellowship and relationship with man and our purpose today is to ask the Holy Spirit to reveal the heart of God in each of us every day.

When Jesus was speaking to the Samaritan woman in John chapter 4, He said to her that the Father is seeking those who will worship Him in spirit and truth. That type of true worship only comes from a heart that is just like His. True and pure worship comes when we spend quality time with the Lord and allowing the Holy Spirit to change our lives daily. He just wants relationship with His children.

As our relationship grows more intimate with God, our worship is no longer just a song that we sing, but it becomes a song of love and adoration from our heart to His. That's the treasure that I desire to have in abundance in my heart today and for eternity, so I encourage you to examine the treasures of your heart and ask Him to fill it with His today!

Day Twenty Two

And to the angel of the church in Philadelphia write, "These things says He who is holy, He who is true, He who has the key of David, He who opens and no one shuts, and shuts and no one opens." (Rev. 3:7)

It's always interesting when reading the 7 letters to the churches in Revelations, how those same letters apply even today in our time and many of our churches as well. The letter to Philadelphia is the only church that does not receive condemnation from God. In fact, I think it's a letter that applies to the body of Christ that is on the edge of a major breakthrough if they follow the instructions of this letter.

Music was King David's access to the presence of God. As you read Rev. 3:7, notice that it says *"He who has the key of David."* What's fascinating to me is that in Isaiah 22:22 it also reads:

> *The key of the house of David I will lay on his shoulder;*
> *so he shall open, and no one shall shut; and he shall shut, and no*
> *one shall open.*

While there are several interpretations of these two particular verses, I propose that the "Key of David" is really the power of true worship. While praying and studying God's Word are both crucial in our daily relationship with the Lord, it's in that place of true worship that God pours out His anointing, presence and glory that changes everything in us and around us.

Worship was the one assignment that Lucifer (satan) was given and he gave it up to pride which led to his downfall. Worship is an area that the enemy hates because he understands its power over him. Why do you think that worship in the church has so much attack against it, worship leaders always under attack, the wars of hymns verses contemporary to let's just do 3 songs so we can get to the "programmed" service? When the people of God gather together in unity and worship until the Lord begins to move then that becomes a major threat to the enemy and then people begin to be set free, healed and deeply ministered too.

As we read Rev. 3:7-13, we see that the "Key of David" which is worship, strengthens you during the hard times. God says that "He opens doors for you that no one can shut because you have stayed faithful and obedient to His Word and He will protect you." Hallelujah, now that's a great place to give Him praise!

I believe that the times we are living in today require us to worship Him despite what the world or enemy says. As we do, God is going to show us and prove to the rest of the world that He is Lord of All!

The following is a passage from the Message Bible and I pray that you will meditate on it and grab that key and worship God and see Him do the impossible through your life and circumstances today.

Revelations 3:7-13

[7] Write this to Philadelphia, to the Angel of the church. The Holy, the True—David's key in his hand, opening doors no one can lock, locking doors no one can open-speaks:

[8] "I see what you've done. Now see what I've done. I've opened a door before you that no one can slam shut. You don't have much strength; I know that; you used what you had to keep my Word. You didn't deny me when times were rough."

[9] "And watch as I take those who call themselves true believers but are nothing of the kind, pretenders whose true membership is in the club of Satan—watch as I strip off their pretensions and they're forced to acknowledge it's you that I've loved."

[10] *"Because you kept my Word in passionate patience, I'll keep you safe in the time of testing that will be here soon, and all over the earth, every man, woman, and child put to the test."*

[11] *"I'm on my way; I'll be there soon. Keep a tight grip on what you have so no one distracts you and steals your crown."*

[12] *"I'll make each conqueror a pillar in the sanctuary of my God, a permanent position of honor. Then I'll write names on you, the pillars: the Name of my God, the Name of God's City—the new Jerusalem coming down out of Heaven—and my new Name."*

[13] *"Are your ears awake? Listen. Listen to the Wind Words, the Spirit blowing through the churches."*

Day Twenty Three

"Praise the LORD! For it is good to sing praises to our God; for it is pleasant, and praise is beautiful." (Psalms 147:1)

One of my top 10 favorite worship songs of all time is "I Sing Praises to Your Name" by my friend Terry MacAlmon, which I love listening to and playing. There are so many wonderful praise and worship songs available to us today by so many gifted and anointed worshipers but there are some songs that God releases that just stand the test of time.

As I was praying this morning, I kept going back into worship with this song and as I prepared to write this today, I just felt like this is a day where God really wants to inhabit our praises unto Him. I don't know about you, but I have been faced with so many challenges and obstacles lately that it would completely boggle the natural mind. Instead of getting down and losing heart I just run to Jesus instead and begin to worship Him and thank Him that He is my Savior, my friend and He is my answer in my time of need.

So in all things, whether good or bad, it is good to sing praises to our God. Psalms 147 from the Message Bible is posted below. After reading it, take a few minutes to sing praises to Jesus and just love on Him and see God respond in such an amazing way of love and grace towards you.

Psalm 147

¹ Hallelujah! It's a good thing to sing praise to our God; praise is beautiful, praise is fitting.
²⁻⁶ God's the one who rebuilds Jerusalem, who re-gathers Israel's scattered exiles. He heals the heartbroken and bandages their wounds. He counts the stars and assigns each a name. Our

Lord is great, with limitless strength; we'll never comprehend what he knows and does. God puts the fallen on their feet again and pushes the wicked into the ditch.

7-11 Sing to God a thanksgiving hymn, play music on your instruments to God, Who fills the sky with clouds, preparing rain for the earth, then turning the mountains green with grass, feeding both cattle and crows. He's not impressed with horsepower; the size of our muscles means little to him. Those who fear God get God's attention; they can depend on his strength.

12-18 Jerusalem, worship God! Zion, praise your God! He made your city secure, he blessed your children among you. He keeps the peace at your borders; he puts the best bread on your tables.
He launches his promises earthward—how swift and sure they come!
He spreads snow like a white fleece, he scatters frost like ashes,
He broadcasts hail like birdseed—who can survive his winter?
Then he gives the command and it all melts; he breathes on winter—suddenly its spring!

19-20 He speaks the same way to Jacob speaks words that work to Israel. He never did this to the other nations; they never heard such commands. Hallelujah!

Day Twenty Four

"Create in me a clean heart, O God, and renew a steadfast spirit within me. Do not cast me away from Your presence, and do not take Your Holy Spirit from me." (Psalms 51:10-11)

I had lunch and wonderful fellowship time with a close friend who is also a Pastor. We were talking about life, ministry, the church, etc... we both were relating to each other how God is so incredible in that He is involved in our daily lives if we let Him.

As our discussion progressed we talked about the journey that God leads us on, the people He places in our lives, and the doors He opens always at the right time. I said that one thing that I have learned the most these past several years since being in fulltime ministry is that to really be used by God, we have to be broken by God.

Doesn't that sound like a great plan for ministry...being broken by God? I love this verse that David declares to God—"Lord, give me a clean heart and do not keep me from your presence and definitely don't take your Holy Spirit away from me." I know that this passage of scripture is talking about having a true heart of repentance but it's also the model of having a continuous heart of God in our everyday lives.

David is the only person in the Bible that God calls "A man after my own heart." In the book of Acts 13, we see Paul talking to the people of Antioch and in verse 22 he makes this statement:

And when He had removed him (King Saul), He raised up for them David as king, to whom also He gave testimony and said, "I have found David the son of Jesse, a man after My own heart, who will do all My will."

I think that is so incredible that David would be recognized by God through the apostle Paul in the New Testament as well. That should speak volumes to where we should be in our walk and our worship to God.

What really grabbed me too was this verse in Psalms 51:17:

The sacrifices of God are a broken spirit, A broken and a contrite heart—These, O God, You will not despise.

What is contrite? Having a broken-heart for sin; deeply affected with grief and sorrow for having offended God; humble; penitent; as a contrite sinner. Not that you have sinned or you are going to sin. It's in that place of saying, "God I can't or won't sin against you because I love you too much to hurt you and/or I will grieve the Holy Spirit deeply.

When you are in that secret place, then God loves to use you for great things. Because you have now placed Him as Lord and King in every area of your life, including over your own will and plans. Paul states that very fact in Acts13:22 when he says that "David was a man after MY own heart—who will do ALL MY WILL!" That's the key to being used greatly by God and becoming a true friend of God. It's a great place to go to and it's an even greater place to stay as well. I encourage you today to become like David, worship Him with all your heart but always remain in a place of brokenness and with a contrite heart and you will become all that He desires you to be.

Day Twenty Five

"If we live in the Spirit, let us also walk in the Spirit."
(Galatians 5:25)

That sounds pretty simple doesn't it? If we live in the Spirit, then let's walk in the Spirit. While God makes everything available to us and He is so good in keeping it simple for us, it still is sometimes harder to do. The key to this whole scripture is "If we live" which means there's either a condition or just a simple choice left up to us to follow or not follow.

So before going further, let's examine it all starting at verse 22-24 which states:

But the fruit of the Spirit is <u>love, joy, peace, longsuffering, kindness, goodness, faithfulness, gentleness, self-control.</u> Against such there is no law. And those who are Christ's have crucified the flesh with its passions and desires.

Paul says that under that law, is there is no law against living a daily life that is filled with heartbeat and attitude of God. (My paraphrasing)

For us to walk in the Spirit daily, requires us to live in His Spirit and when that takes place we are going to be a mirror image of Christ here on earth. As we begin to exemplify the fruit of the Spirit—*"love, joy, peace, longsuffering, kindness, goodness, faithfulness, gentleness, self-control"*—in our attitudes, lives and interactions with people, we will be walking evangelists that will show them that Christ is real and that He loves them so very much.

As always with God, there's another bonus added to everything He does for us. Paul states in verse 24 that as we allow the "fruit of the

Spirit" to be active daily in our life, we are then living and walking in the Spirit and now our "fleshly passions and desires" have been crucified with Christ. I love how God always wants to do more for us. God is in the business of changing us every day to be more like Him.

Lord I pray that everyone reading this now will be filled with Your Spirit. I ask that the fruit of the spirit (God's very character) would become so ingrained in the very DNA of their heart, spirit and life that people everywhere would be drawn to You. Those that have never been ministered to before with the heart of the Father, I pray that You would touch their lives and that many will be healed in every way and come to know Jesus by His spirit that lives and walks in each of us today. In Jesus name, Amen!

Day Twenty Six

When all the Israelites saw the fire coming down and the glory of the LORD above the temple, they knelt on the pavement with their faces to the ground, and they worshiped and gave thanks to the LORD, saying, "He is good; his love endures forever." (2 Chronicles 7:3)

2 Chronicles: Chapters 5-7 are some of my favorite chapters from the Old Testament about worship. King Solomon understood during these chapters that bringing God the best worship was vital for His calling as a King and for the people of Israel.

In chapter 5 we see that as the worshipers began to worship God that the "glory cloud" came in so strong no one could stand to minister anymore. Wow, I absolutely love that. As we enter into chapter 7, Solomon has finished praying to God when a "fire" came down from heaven and consumed the offerings and the sacrifices, and the glory came again and filled the temple. The priests could NOT enter because of the glory of the Lord filled the house. I don't know about you but I want to experience that every time we come together to worship.

So how do we have this in our lives or in our services today? I believe that there are some valuable nuggets from here to learn. The first thing is when we gather to worship corporately, there has to be unity together and with God's spirit. In Chapter 5:13 it says:

> *indeed it came to pass, when the trumpeters and singers <u>were as one</u>, to make <u>one </u>sound to be heard in praising and thanking the LORD, and when they lifted up their voice with the trumpets and cymbals and instruments of music, and praised the LORD....*

The second thing is this, if we truly want the "fire of God" then what kind of offerings and sacrifices are we bringing Him today? There's a classis worship song that says "We bring the sacrifice of Praise...." but do we really? This is much a challenge to you as it is me. I will say this; I am praying and asking God for it all the time. I want to offer Him the best with everything that I have and to see what happened in Chapters 5 & 7 come to pass when I worship Him. I believe that if we can make that type of covenant with God as Solomon did, then He will be more than able to make it come to pass in our lives as well.

One last thing I observed here as well, later in Chapter 7:14, we see God telling Solomon how he will confirm His covenant with Him. This passage is well known but is usually spoken from Isaiah 43:7 which reads:

> *...if my people, who are called by my name, will humble themselves and pray and seek my face and turn from their wicked ways, then will I hear from heaven and will forgive their sin and will heal their land.*

The bottom line is this; we want to see a move of God. We hunger for more of His presence and glory and want to be in services where the anointing of God is so strong that no one can even move. However, the key to seeing a real revival or a move of God comes from His people humbling themselves and seeking His face in prayer for families, towns, cities, states, countries and beyond.

I want to challenge you to become a shaker of heaven and earth today through prayer and worship. It doesn't happen overnight, but if we will persistently go after the promises of God's Word and authority, worship Him and pray with His heart—what a day that will be when we gather together in unity. Offering God our best so that His fire and glory will come and fill our churches, homes and lives and the world will know that our God reigns!

Day Twenty Seven

"Rejoice in the Lord always. I will say it again: Rejoice!"
(Philippians 4:4)

Let us rejoice in our Lord and Savior, the one who paid the price for our salvation and bore every sickness, disease, bondage and everything else we were not meant to have or take on. Jesus Christ is the same yesterday, today and forever in that He is so in love with you, just as you are. I love Him because He not only saved, delivered and healed me but He placed His love in me with a purpose of worshiping Him in spirit and in truth. Praise the Lord!

When reading Philippians 4, I noticed some great scripture passages that I would like for you to read and let those verses get into your heart and spirit since the Holy Spirit wrote these to you and me, personally. That's how awesome our Lord is!

- *Do not be anxious about anything, but in everything, by prayer and petition, with thanksgiving, present your requests to God. And the peace of God, which transcends all understanding, will guard your hearts and your minds in Christ Jesus. Finally, brothers, whatever is true, whatever is noble, whatever is right, whatever is pure, whatever is lovely, whatever is admirable—if anything is excellent or praiseworthy—think about such things.* **(Philippians 4:6-8)**

- *I can do everything through him who gives me strength.* **(Philippians 4:13)**

- *And my God will meet all your needs according to his glorious riches in Christ Jesus.* **(Philippians 4:19)**

After reading just these 3 passages I have highlighted for you, I can only rejoice in all that He has done and will do on our behalf. Thank you so much Jesus for being such an incredible friend and Savior in our everyday life. What can I say except thank you and that I love you for loving me before I was even created. Take time to rejoice in all He has done and is about to do on your behalf.

Day Twenty Eight

And He said, "My Presence will go with you, and I will give you rest." (Exodus 33:14)

I want to share with you that God's presence is so important in each and every day. When you and I gave our hearts to Jesus Christ, we were immediately given the best of the best from heaven—the Holy Spirit.

It's through the Holy Spirit, God's presence, who gives us that perfect peace and rest no matter what we're going through. There is a scripture that comes to mind as to who we are in Christ from 1 Peter 2:9-10:

> *But you are a chosen generation, a royal priesthood, a holy nation, His own special people, that you may proclaim the praises of Him who called you out of darkness into His marvelous light; who once were not a people but are now the people of God, who had not obtained mercy but now have obtained mercy.*

That's in essence what God was saying to Moses in Exodus 33:13-17 which says:

> *"Now therefore, I pray, if I have found grace in Your sight, show me now Your way, that I may know You and that I may find grace in Your sight. And consider that <u>this nation is Your people</u>." And He said, "My Presence will go with you, and I will give you rest." Then he said to Him, "If Your Presence does not go with us, do not bring us up from here. For how then will it be known that Your people and I have found grace in Your sight, except You go with us? So we shall be separate, Your people and I, from all the people who are upon the face of the earth." So the LORD said to Moses, "I will also do this thing that you have spoken; for you have found grace in My sight, <u>and I know you by name</u>."*

It is so assuring to me that I can rest in His presence because I am part of the chosen generation, a holy nation (His Kingdom), a royal priesthood and He knows you and me by name—Praise God!

There's a song titled "In The Presence of Jehovah" by Geron Davis which is a powerful song, especially the chorus that captures what can happen when we are in the presence of our King! If you will spend some time in the presence of the Lord, you will see the troubles begin to vanish and who knows, God may even surprise you with more of His goodness just because He loves you so much.

Day Twenty Nine

indeed it came to pass, when the trumpeters and singers were as one, to make one sound to be word heard in praising and thanking the LORD, and when they lifted up their voice with the trumpets and cymbals and instruments of music, and praised the LORD, saying: "For He is good, For His mercy endures forever," that the house, the house of the LORD, was filled with a cloud, so that the priests could not continue ministering because of the cloud; for the glory of the LORD filled the house of God. (2 Chronicles 5:13-14)

In March, 2010 I was being interviewed on an online radio talk show and the discussion was on "The Power of Worship!" During the discussion I talked about the glory of God. I believe that the glory (weightiness of His presence) is essential in our worship services today. As you read the passage above, that when they were as "ONE" in not only their sound, but in the spirit of true worship, the presence of God filled the temple and no one could stand or minister.

True worship, as Jesus talked about in John 4, is more than just a song or how great we can sound. True worship always begins from your heart to His heart. Talents and gifts are really ineffective without the anointing of the Holy Spirit.

There's more to examine, so let's read Chapter 6:1-2 which then Solomon, after this incredible event, says the following:

"The LORD said He would dwell in the dark cloud. I have surely built You an exalted house, and a place for You to dwell in forever."

What are you building today for the Holy One of Israel? What habitation are you creating in your life and heart so that the presence of the Lord can dwell in forever?

Let's continue on as there's more here. In Chapter 6 of 2 Chronicles we see King Solomon giving a powerful prayer, blessings, honor and worship to the Lord as he dedicates the temple.

As we enter Chapter 7, let's read verses 1-3:

When Solomon had finished praying, fire came down from heaven and consumed the burnt offering and the sacrifices; and the glory of the LORD filled the temple. And the priests could not enter the house of the LORD, because the glory of the LORD had filled the LORD's house. When all the children of Israel saw how the fire came down, and the glory of the LORD on the temple, they bowed their faces to the ground on the pavement, and worshiped and praised the LORD, saying:

"For He is good, For His mercy endures forever."

I absolutely love this passage in Chapter 7. What an example of worship, so moving the heart of God that He sends the "fire" and then His "presence" fills the temple so that now, no one could enter the temple. As this scene unfolds, the children of Israel become prostrate before a Holy God. With their faces to the ground they worshiped and praised Him.

I am in awe just imagining this whole event in my mind right now as I write this. My heart is burning for this to become not only a reality today, but a regular occurrence when we gather together in unity, to worship Him from our hearts. I pray that it will become the burning cry of your heart today.

Day Thirty

Do you want some keys to being a strong believer? Then let's examine three men in the bible who had valuable keys in being used mightily by God.

Joseph—*The LORD was with Joseph, and he was a successful man; and he was in the house of his master the Egyptian. And his master saw that the LORD was with him and that the LORD made all he did to prosper in his hand. So Joseph found favor in his sight, and served him. Then he made him overseer of his house, and all that he had he put under his authority. So it was, from the time that he had made him overseer of his house and all that he had, that the LORD blessed the Egyptian's house for Joseph's sake; and the blessing of the LORD was on all that he had in the house and in the field.* (Genesis 39:2-5)

Daniel—*Then the king instructed Ashpenaz, the master of his eunuchs, to bring some of the children of Israel and some of the king's descendants and some of the nobles, young men in whom there was no blemish, but good-looking, gifted in all wisdom, possessing knowledge and quick to understand, who had ability to serve in the king's palace, and whom they might teach the language and literature of the Chaldeans.* (Daniel 1: 3-4)

Then the king interviewed them, and among them all none was found like Daniel, Hananiah, Mishael, and Azariah; therefore they served before the king. And in all matters of wisdom and understanding about which the king examined them, he found them ten times better than all the magicians and astrologers who were in all his realm. (Daniel 1:19-20)

Stephen—*"Therefore, brethren, seek out from among you seven men of good reputation, full of the Holy Spirit and wisdom, whom we may appoint over this business; but we will give ourselves continually to prayer and to the ministry of the Word." And the saying pleased the whole multitude. And they chose Stephen, a man full of faith and the Holy Spirit.... (Acts 6:3-5) And Stephen, full of faith and power, did great wonders and signs among the people. (Acts 6:8)*

Valuable keys to being used mightily by God:
1. Humility
2. Integrity
3. Godly Character
4. Wisdom
5. Love & Compassion

There's a saying that goes "it's not how you start but how you finish" but I say if we can start out with these 5 keys we will also finish the race strongly and see many come into the kingdom of God.

About the Author

For the past 15 years, Damon Stuart has been using the gifts the Lord placed on his life to lead people into His presence. Before going into full time ministry Damon started out as a worship leader in a very small church in the Northwest suburbs of Chicago. One of Damon's favorite bible verses was really a true representation of where the Lord was launching him at that time. It states in Zech. 4:10 "Do not despise these small beginnings, for the Lord rejoices to see the work begin..."

Damon accepted the call from the Lord and the journey began for him to not be just a worship leader but a presence seeker of God. His passion and desire is to take you into that intimate place of worship that ushers you in the very throne room of God. As Damon says often, there is nothing better than being in the presence of the Lord.

Damon's call to worship and ministry began when he was a child. His parents, who are also pastors, played a significant role in his passion for Christ and for the church. Going to church, worship music and biblical teaching was part of his life while growing up. In his school years Damon took piano lessons and was involved in band and show choir, not realizing that God was preparing him for what he would be doing later in life. Through the years, God has touched Damon's life many times, revealing the Fathers heart with amazing love, forgiveness and miracles that would set him on a course for what God would have him accomplish for the kingdom.

Damon has ministered throughout the U.S. and internationally as a worship leader, psalmist and evangelist. He has also appeared and ministered on several Christian television and radio programs. As a worship leader, his desire is to bring people into the deeper realms of God's glory through worship. As Damon ministers, the healing, prophetic anointing and manifested presence of God takes place.

Damon's heart burns passionately to release the word of God as an evangelist, seeing the Kingdom of God expanded throughout the nations. His desire is to see the book Acts become just as real today for the church than ever before. His passion is to take you into a deeper relationship with the Father through worship and God's word. He is one who preaches the word with power and authority, allowing the Holy Spirit to move and transform your life so that you will never be the same again!

Damon is a songwriter, recording artist, conference speaker, teacher and author and has served as a worship pastor/leader for over 15 years. He also taught a college course series on worship at Christian Life College in Mt. Prospect, IL. Damon resides with his wife and two children in the northwest suburbs of Chicago, IL. Damon is Ordained through White Horse Christian Center.

If you would like to invite Damon to come and minster at your church, conference, crusade or event visit the website at damonstuart.com or email us at info@damonstuart.com

CPSIA information can be obtained at www.ICGtesting.com
Printed in the USA
LVOW08s2025280615

444026LV00001B/2/P